I0510556

This Journal Belongs
To:

____

Published by Daily
Jotting

www.ingramcontent.com/pod-product-compliance
Lightning Source LLC
Chambersburg PA
CBHW030945240526
45463CB00016B/1965
* 9 7 8 1 6 9 2 1 3 4 1 0 5 *